CAREER EXPLORATION

Dental Assistant

by Rosemary Wallner

Consultant:
Jennifer K. Blake, CDA, EFDA
ADAA Education Manager
American Dental Assistants Association

CAPSTONE BOOKS

an imprint of Capstone Press
Mankato, Minnesota

Capstone Books are published by Capstone Press
151 Good Counsel Drive, P.O. Box 669, Mankato, Minnesota 56002
http://www.capstone-press.com

Library of Congress Cataloging-in-Publication Data
Wallner, Rosemary, 1964–
    Dental assistant/by Rosemary Wallner.
    p. cm.—(Career exploration)
    Includes bibliographical references and index.
    Summary: Introduces the career of dental assistant, providing information
about educational requirements, duties, the workplace, salary, employment outlook,
and possible future positions.
    ISBN 0-7368-0593-1
    1. Dental assistants—Vocational guidance. 2. Dental assistants—Vocational
guidance—Juvenile literature. [1. Dental assistants—Vocational guidance.
2. Vocational guidance.] I. Title. II. Series.
RK60.5 .W35 2001
617.6'0233—dc21   00-021542

Editorial Credits
Leah K. Pockrandt, editor; Steve Christensen, cover designer; Kia Bielke, production
    designer and illustrator; Heidi Schoof and Kim Danger, photo researchers

Photo Credits
Art Womack, 40
bachmann/Pictor, 9
Daniel Grogan/Pictor, 37
David F. Clobes, 13, 16, 18, 39
International Stock/Hal Kern, 21
Jeff Greenberg/Pictor, 29
Leslie O'Shaughnessy, 6, 10, 22, 30, 33, 34, 46
Ron Holt/Pictor, 14
Unicorn Stock Photos, 26

1 2 3 4 5 6 06 05 04 03 02 01

Table of Contents

Fast Facts

Career Title	Dental Assistant
O*NET Number	66002
DOT Cluster (Dictionary of Occupational Titles)	Professional, technical, and managerial occupations
DOT Number	079.361-018
GOE Number (Guide for Occupational Exploration)	10.03.02
NOC Number (National Occupational Classification-Canada)	341
Salary Range (U.S. Bureau of Labor Statistics and Human Resources Development Canada, late 1990s figures)	U.S.: $14,685 to $32,677 Canada: $18,400 to $46,500 (Canadian dollars)
Minimum Educational Requirements	U.S.: high school education; vocational or technical program or certificate preferred Canada: high school education; vocational or technical program or certificate preferred
Certification/Licensing Requirements	U.S.: varies by duties and state Canada: varies by duties and province

Subject Knowledge

Medicine and dentistry; clerical

Personal Abilities/Skills

Want to help people; work with the young, elderly, sick, or disabled; understand and follow instructions exactly; use arms, eyes, hands, and fingers with skill; talk and relate to people in need

Job Outlook

U.S.: faster than average growth
Canada: fair

Personal Interests

Humanitarian: interest in helping others with their mental, spiritual, social, physical, or vocational needs

Similar Types of Jobs

Medical assistant; physical therapy assistant; occupational therapy assistant; pharmacy technician or assistant; veterinary technician

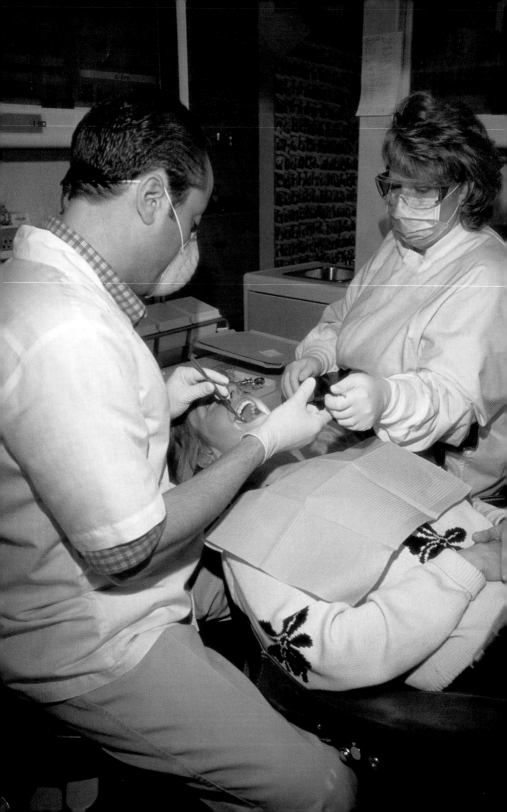

Chapter 1

Dental Assistant

Dental assistants work with dentists. Dental assistants help dentists work on patients and help make the patients comfortable.

Dental assistants perform a variety of tasks. They assist dentists with dental procedures. They also may perform clerical duties. They may answer phones, make appointments, and greet patients.

Working in Treatment Rooms

Dentists perform procedures in treatment rooms. Dental assistants prepare these rooms for dentists. They sterilize dental instruments. They clean the instruments to remove any germs. They then place the instruments on trays. They organize the tools so the tools are where the dentists need them.

Dental assistants help dentists during dental procedures. Dental assistants work chairside. They

Dental assistants help dentists during dental procedures.

work next to patients and dentists. Assistants hand dentists the proper dental instruments. They also keep the patients' mouths dry and clean.

Dental assistants help keep patients calm and relaxed. Dental assistants talk quietly to patients. Procedures are easier when patients are calm.

Dental assistants have other duties after dentists are finished with procedures. They answer patients' questions. Dental assistants clean treatment rooms after patients leave. They also prepare instruments and rooms for other patients.

Working in the Laboratory
Some dental assistants work in dental laboratories. These labs are located in dental offices. Labs contain special dental equipment. In labs, dental assistants may make casts of patients' teeth. To make a cast, a dental assistant first takes an impression or mold of a patient's teeth. The assistant then pours a soft material into the mold. When the material hardens, the assistant removes the cast from the mold.

Dental assistants may have other duties in labs. They may clean and polish dentures. These false teeth fit into people's mouths.

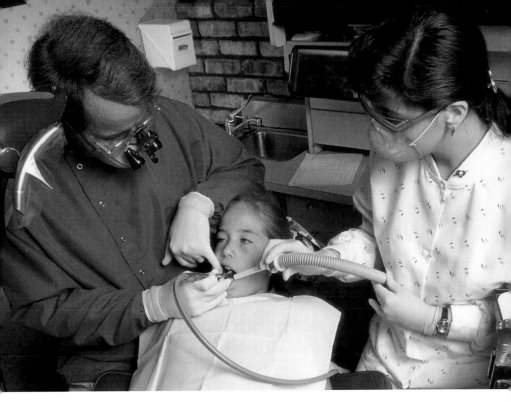

Dental assistants work chairside.

Working with X-ray Equipment

Some dental assistants take and develop radiographs. Radiographs are more commonly called x-rays. They are photographs of teeth produced by radioactive light beams and special film. Dentists use x-rays to look for trouble spots such as cavities. These holes in teeth are caused by tooth decay. Dentists also use x-rays to check tooth growth underneath the gums.

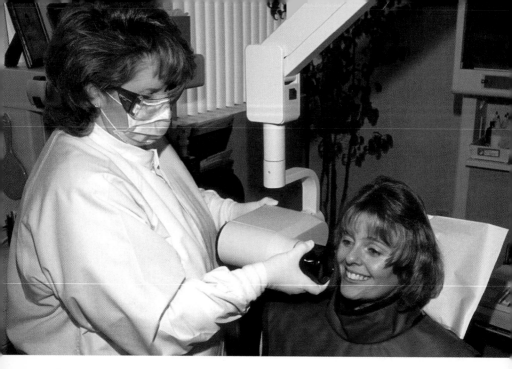

Some dental assistants use x-ray equipment.

Dental assistants usually take patients' x-rays at the beginning of exams. The dental assistant places a shield over the patient's body to block out harmful radiation rays. This shield is made of a metal called lead. The dental assistant then places small, hard pieces of paper next to the patient's teeth. These pieces of paper contain the film. The assistant steps out of the room to turn on the x-ray machine. The machine takes pictures of the teeth. The assistant then removes the film and processes it in the lab.

Not all dental assistants use x-ray equipment. In some states, dental assistants must take additional training and pass a test to take and process x-rays. A state licensing board oversees this test. Dental assistants receive a certificate when they pass this test.

In Canada, dental assistants are either level 1 or level 2 dental assistants. Level 1 dental assistants only assist the dentist chairside. Level 2 dental assistants perform additional duties. These include taking x-rays, making casts, applying fluoride, and performing other intra-oral duties.

Clerical Duties

Some dental assistants perform clerical duties. They call patients to schedule and confirm appointments. They answer phone calls from patients who want to schedule appointments. Dental assistants also greet patients as they arrive at the office or clinic.

Dental assistants often use computers to perform clerical duties. They keep track of patient records and dental supplies using computers. Dental assistants also use computers to send bills and record payments.

Tools and Equipment

Dental assistants handle many dental instruments. They must know when dentists need each instrument. For example, dental assistants must give dentists the correct handpieces during dental procedures. Dentists use these long, thin devices to hold dental instruments. Handpieces are connected to a motor that turns the end of the handpiece.

The end of each handpiece holds a different instrument. For example, the end of one handpiece may have a polishing stone. This instrument is used to smooth a tooth's surface. The end of another handpiece may have a cutting bur. Dentists use a bur to cut and shape teeth during restoration work. This handpiece is commonly called a drill. Dentists alter or repair the appearance of patients' teeth during restoration work.

Dental assistants use tools such as suction devices and air and water syringes. Suction devices are electric devices with long tubes attached to them. Dental assistants use the tubes to remove water and saliva from patients' mouths. They also use suction devices to remove tooth and filling materials when dentists fill cavities. A syringe is

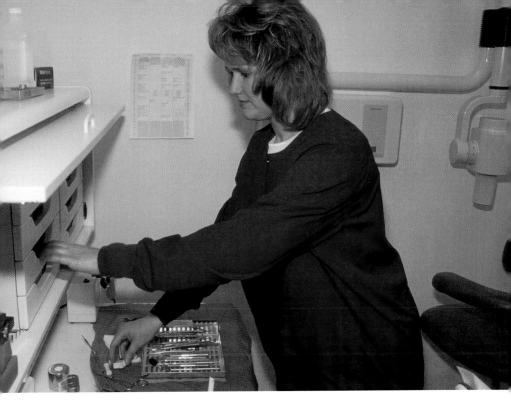

Dental assistants handle many dental instruments.

a long tube with a nozzle at one end. Dental
assistants use water syringes to rinse patients'
mouths and teeth. Dental assistants use air
syringes to dry tooth surfaces.

Dental assistants work with dental cement
and filling materials. Dentists use these
materials to fill cavities. Dental assistants must
prepare these materials. They must know when
to hand them to dentists during procedures.

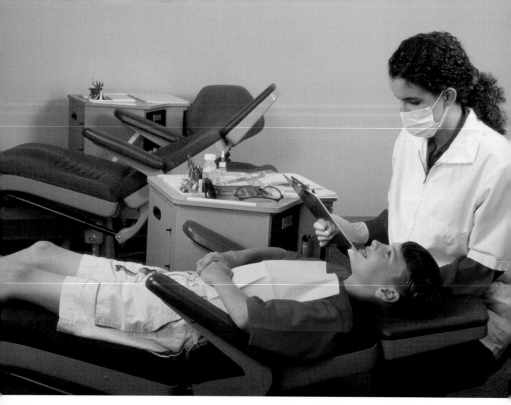

Some dental assistants work in orthodontic clinics.

Infection Control

Dental assistants must protect themselves, dentists, and patients from infectious diseases. These diseases can be spread from one person to another through germs or viruses. Dental assistants wear gloves, masks, and eyewear to help prevent the spread of these diseases.

Dental assistants must clean the treatment room and equipment. This includes sterilizing all the instruments before they are used.

Work Settings

Most dental assistants work in private practices. Some dental assistants work in individual dental practices. Other dental assistants work in group practices or clinics.

Some dental assistants work in specialty practices. These practices include oral surgery, orthodontics, endodontics, or pediatric dentistry. Oral surgeons often remove patients' teeth. Orthodontists straighten patients' teeth. Pediatric dentists specialize in treating children. Endodontists perform root canal treatments.

Dental assistants also work in other settings. Some work at dental schools or government hospitals. Other dental assistants work in state or local public health departments or clinics. Still other dental assistants work for dental insurance companies.

Most dental assistants work a set number of hours each week. Most dental assistants work from 32 to 40 hours each week. Some dental assistants work on Saturdays or evenings. Some patients' schedules do not allow them to have appointments during regular business hours. Many dental practices or clinics offer weekend or evening appointment times for these patients.

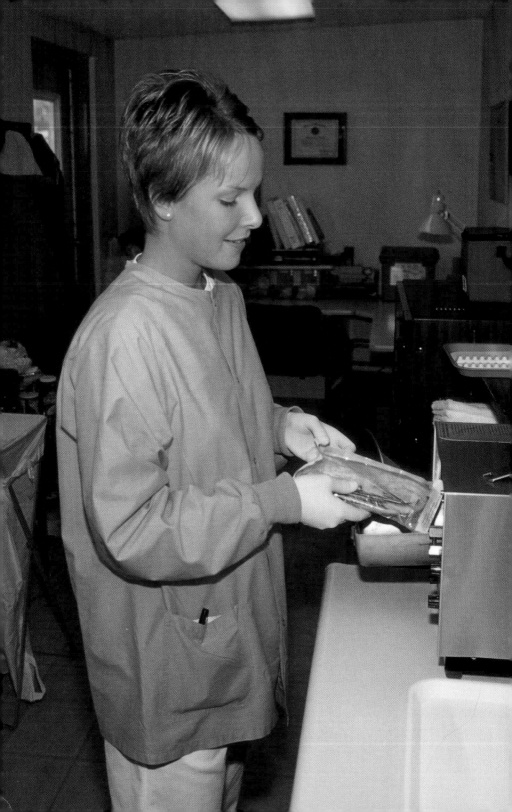

Chapter 2

Day-to-Day Activities

Dental assistants perform a variety of tasks throughout the day. The type of work they perform depends on the dental needs of each patient. Dental assistants perform tasks before, during, and after patient appointments. The tasks also vary depending on where dental assistants work.

Before the Dentists Arrive

Dental assistants perform several tasks before patient appointments. They prepare the instruments and equipment. Dental assistants first sterilize all tools that dentists use on patients. They then prepare trays of instruments for the dentists. Dental assistants

Dental assistants sterilize all dental instruments before appointments.

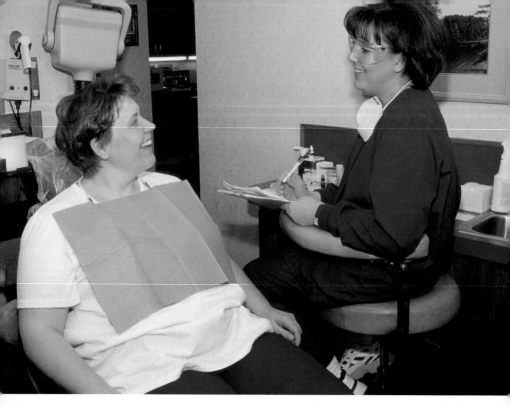

Dental assistants ask patients about their medical and dental histories.

make sure that enough instruments are cleaned and ready.

Next, dental assistants work with the patients. They greet patients and show them to the treatment room. They seat the patient in the dental chair. They also put a bib on the patient. The bibs help keep patients' clothes clean. Some dental assistants take x-rays if they are needed.

Dental assistants may ask patients about their medical and dental histories. They need to know if the patients are taking any medications or have any health problems. Dental assistants ask about the patients' last dental visit. Dental assistants also ask patients about the reason for the dental visit. Dental assistants write down this information in the patients' charts.

Patients sometimes are upset or afraid about their upcoming dental procedures. Dental assistants offer comfort to these patients. They help patients feel relaxed. They answer any questions the patients may have about the procedures.

During the Appointment

During procedures, dental assistants try to think about the dentist's and patient's needs. They hand instruments to the dentist. They keep the patient's mouth dry and clear by using suction or other devices.

Dental assistants follow the dentist's instructions. Dental assistants may prepare filling material for cavities. The dental assistant hands the material to the dentist when the dentist asks for it. Dental assistants also may take impressions of patients' teeth to make dental casts.

Dental assistants must keep patients relaxed. They know it is easier for dentists to work on calm, relaxed patients. Adult patients sometimes are nervous. Dental assistants may describe what the dentist is doing during the procedure. They also may distract the patient's attention away from the procedure. For example, they may ask about the patient's hobbies. Younger patients sometimes are frightened. Dental assistants may let young patients hold toothbrushes or small toys to distract them.

After the Appointment

Dental assistants often talk with patients after procedures are over. They tell patients how to care for fillings. Dental assistants remind patients how to care for their teeth. They review

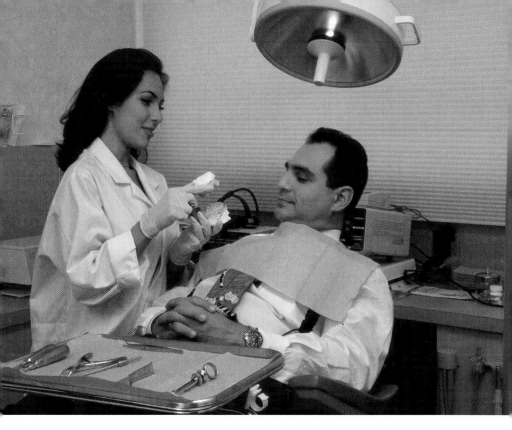

Some dental assistants make casts of patients' teeth.

how to properly brush and floss. They also may schedule follow-up appointments with patients.

Dental assistants perform other tasks after procedures. They write notes about the appointment in the patient's chart. They sterilize any instruments used and prepare trays for other patients.

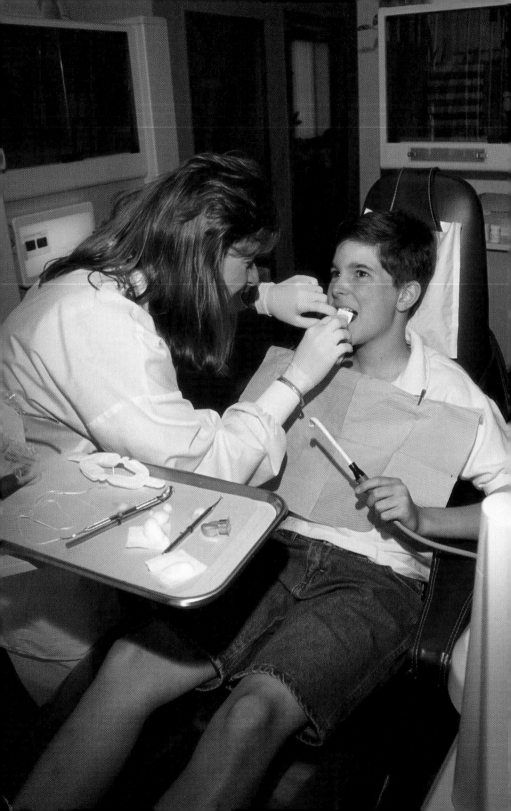

Chapter 3

The Right Candidate

Dental assistants need a variety of skills. They need to work well with people. They must be dependable. They also need to have good hand-eye coordination.

Interests and Abilities

Dental assistants should enjoy working closely with people. They also should want to help people. They need to make sure patients are as comfortable as possible.

Dental assistants must be able to work with different types of people. They often work with children, the elderly, and people with disabilities. Dental assistants must be able to put all types of people at ease.

Dental assistants must have strong verbal and written communication skills. They must be able

Dental assistants should enjoy working with a variety of people.

Skills

Workplace Skills   Yes / No

Resources:
- Assign use of time .... ☑ ☐
- Assign use of money .... ☐ ☑
- Assign use of material and facility resources .... ☑ ☐
- Assign use of human resources .... ☑ ☐

Interpersonal Skills:
- Take part as a member of a team .... ☑ ☐
- Teach others .... ☑ ☐
- Serve clients/customers .... ☑ ☐
- Show leadership .... ☑ ☐
- Work with others to arrive at a decision .... ☑ ☐
- Work with a variety of people .... ☑ ☐

Information:
- Acquire and judge information .... ☑ ☐
- Understand and follow legal requirements .... ☑ ☐
- Organize and maintain information .... ☑ ☐
- Understand and communicate information .... ☑ ☐
- Use computers to process information .... ☑ ☐

Systems:
- Identify, understand, and work with systems .... ☑ ☐
- Understand environmental, social, political, economic,
  or business systems .... ☑ ☐
- Oversee and correct system performance .... ☐ ☑
- Improve and create systems .... ☐ ☑

Technology:
- Select technology .... ☐ ☑
- Apply technology to task .... ☑ ☐
- Maintain and troubleshoot technology .... ☐ ☑

Foundation Skills

Basic Skills:
- Read .... ☑ ☐
- Write .... ☑ ☐
- Do arithmetic and math .... ☑ ☐
- Speak and listen .... ☑ ☐

Thinking Skills:
- Learn .... ☑ ☐
- Reason .... ☑ ☐
- Think creatively .... ☑ ☐
- Make decisions .... ☑ ☐
- Solve problems .... ☑ ☐

Personal Qualities:
- Take individual responsibility .... ☑ ☐
- Have self-esteem and self-management .... ☑ ☐
- Be sociable .... ☑ ☐
- Be fair, honest, and sincere .... ☑ ☐

to speak calmly to patients. They must remain calm even if the patient is upset. Dental assistants need to be able to clearly explain dental procedures to patients. They use writing skills to keep accurate charts and patient records.

Work Styles

Dental assistants are part of dental health care teams. These teams include dentists and dental hygienists. Some dental assistants also work with dental laboratory technicians. These people make dentures and crowns. A crown replaces a badly damaged tooth. Dental assistants must work well with other team members.

Dental assistants must be able to understand and follow dentists' instructions exactly. They may hand dentists certain tools. They may find patients' x-rays. They may help dentists fill cavities. Dentists and patients rely on dental assistants to do their job well.

Dental assistants must work quickly and skillfully. They need to have good hand-eye coordination. Dental assistants also must be careful and gentle to avoid hurting people while they work.

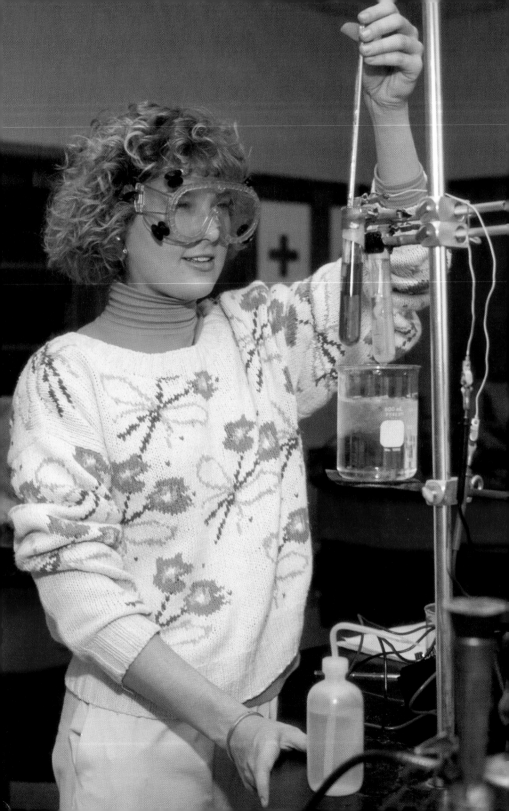

Chapter 4

Preparing for the Career

People who want to become dental assistants usually complete approved dental assisting programs at technical or community colleges. These programs take from nine months to one year to complete. Students also may be required to take a certification or registering exam after they complete school.

High School Education
Students who want to become dental assistants should take a variety of classes. These include science classes such as biology and chemistry. Students study living things in biology classes. In chemistry classes, students learn how

Students who want to become dental assistants should take chemistry classes.

different chemicals react to each other and other elements.

Students also should take health, communication, and computer classes. Dental assistants need to communicate with dentists, patients, and other staff members. They also may use computers to record patients' information.

Students should work hard in their classes. Students may need good grades in science and English to get into some dental assistant training programs.

Students can benefit from watching dental assistants at work. Students may be able to visit a local dental office. These students can watch dental assistants perform their duties.

Post-Secondary Education

The best way to become a dental assistant is to complete a training program. Most dentists prefer to hire dental assistants who have completed a training program. These dental assistants receive a certificate, diploma, or degree.

High school graduates in North America may attend dental assistant training programs.

Students who want to become dental assistants should take a variety of science classes.

Students receive a certificate or diploma after completing most programs. In the United States, students who attend a community or junior college receive an associate's degree. Students earn an associate's degree in about two years.

Dental assistant programs last about nine months to one year. These programs include science classes such as dental anatomy and pathology. Dental anatomy is the study of the teeth and mouth. Dental pathology is the study

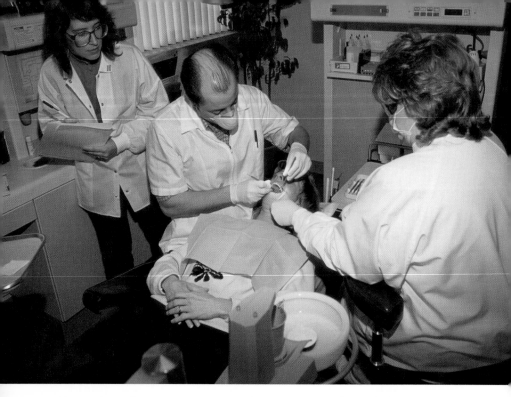

Dental assistants may receive on-the-job training.

of diseases that affect the mouth. Students also take classes in chairside assisting and office management. Some students may gain experience by working at clinics or dental offices.

In Canada, level 2 dental assistant students must complete training at a college or technical school. Level 1 dental assistants can later receive the level 2 training.

Dental assistants in some areas of North America can begin their careers without a degree.

In these areas, high school graduates may receive on-the-job training. These dental assistants are trained by experienced assistants or dentists. The assistants learn to perform specific tasks at a dental office or clinic. They also may need to take additional training outside the office.

Students in the United States may need to take additional classes to perform specialized tasks. Most dental assistants who take x-rays need special training. These students then receive a certificate to show they are able to take and process x-rays. In Canada, dental assistants need level 2 training to take x-rays.

Licensing

Some states and provinces require dental assistants to be licensed. Others require successful completion of a radiology examination. Dental assistants who take x-rays need to complete a radiology examination.

Dental assistants must pass an exam to become certified. In the United States, the Dental Assisting National Board (DANB) oversees the exam. In Canada, the National Dental Assisting Examining Board (NDAEB) oversees the exam. Dental assistants who pass the exam show that they are prepared to assist in dental care. These dental assistants are Certified Dental Assistants. They then may use the initials CDA after their name.

In the United States, dental assistants take the exam after completing an approved dental assisting program. Dental assistants who have been trained on the job take the exam after they have worked for two years.

In Canada, dental assistants may obtain certification through the NDAEB. Certification is not required in Canada. But certified dental assistants are able to work in certain provinces more easily than non-certified dental assistants.

Continuing Education

Dental assistants must continue to upgrade their skills. Dental assistants who are CDAs must take refresher classes each year. They also can prove their skills through retesting.

Many dental assistants join professional organizations. Assistants in the United States may join the American Dental Assistants Association. Canadian assistants may join

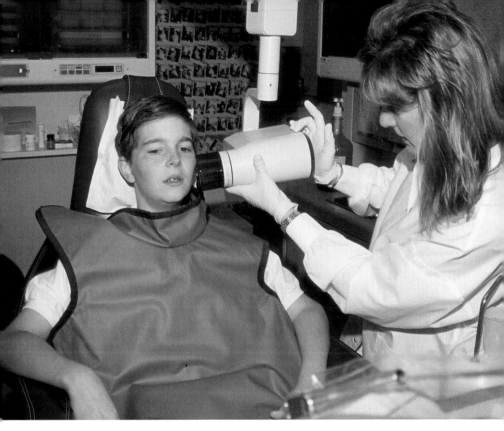

Dental assistants who take x-rays need to complete radiology training.

provincial associations and the Canadian Dental Assistants' Association. Dental assisting students also may join the provincial and national associations. Professional organizations keep members informed about changes in the career. They also offer continuing education classes and address issues that concern dental assistants.

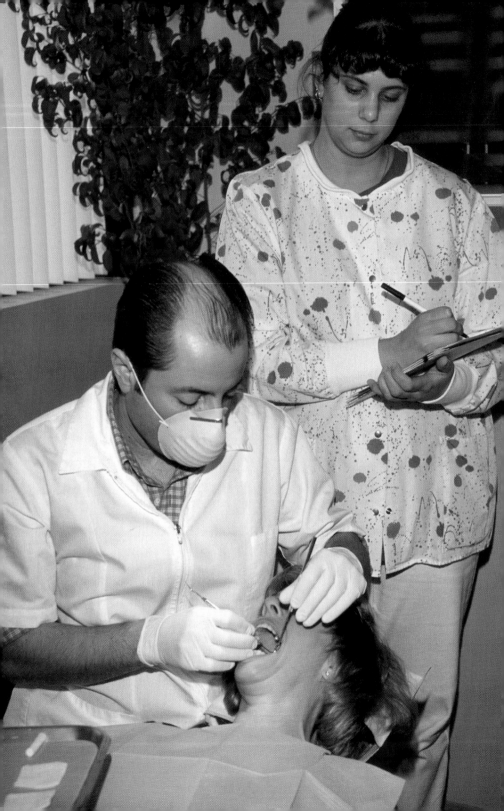

Chapter 5

The Market

The job outlook for dental assistants is good. Some dentists are hiring more dental assistants to perform a variety of tasks. This allows dentists to spend most of their time on more difficult procedures.

Salary

Salaries vary depending on dental assistants' tasks. Dental assistants who are certified to work on x-ray equipment may earn more than uncertified assistants do. Salaries also vary with dental assistants' experience and education.

In the United States, dental assistants earn between $14,685 and $32,677 per year. The average yearly salary for full-time dental assistants is $22,630.

Dental assistants perform a variety of tasks.

In Canada, dental assistants earn between $18,400 and $46,500 per year. But this salary range is based on a group of people in other occupations. This group includes nurses' aides, orthopedic technologists, and pharmacy assistants. The average yearly salary for professionals in this group is about $33,500.

Job Outlook

In the United States, dental assistants will have many job opportunities. The job outlook for dental assistants is expected to have much faster than average growth. Most of these job openings will be in entry-level positions.

More dental assistants will be needed as dentists become busier. Today, people are taking better care of their teeth. They visit dentists more often. Dentists need more

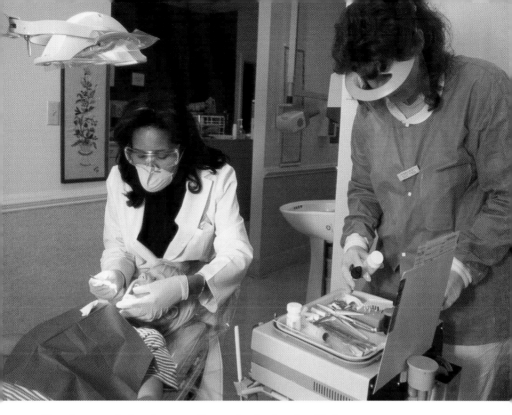

Dental assistants continue to help dentists serve more patients.

dental assistants to help them serve more patients.

In Canada, the job outlook for dental assistants is fair. Government cutbacks in health care may decrease jobs for dental assistants.

Advancement Opportunities

Dental assistants may advance in several ways. Those who work in small dental offices may move to larger dental offices. Dental assistants may have more responsibilities at larger offices. They may be able to assist with more exams or perform more lab work. Dental assistants also may earn higher salaries in larger offices.

Some dental assistants return to school to become dental hygienists. These dental care workers clean and polish patients' teeth. Dental hygienists must graduate from an accredited dental hygiene school. They must pass a written and clinical exam. They then earn a license to work with dentists.

Some dental assistants become teachers. But these people need additional education to do these jobs. They may need to earn a bachelor's degree from a college or university. People earn this degree by completing a course of study. Most people earn this degree in about four years.

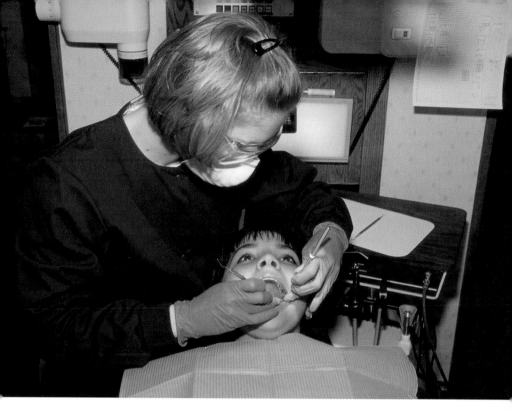

Some dental assistants may return to school to become dental hygienists.

Dental assistants who teach may work at technical or vocational schools, colleges, or universities. They teach dental assisting classes and work in program administration. Program administration workers help design a school's course of study for dental assistants.

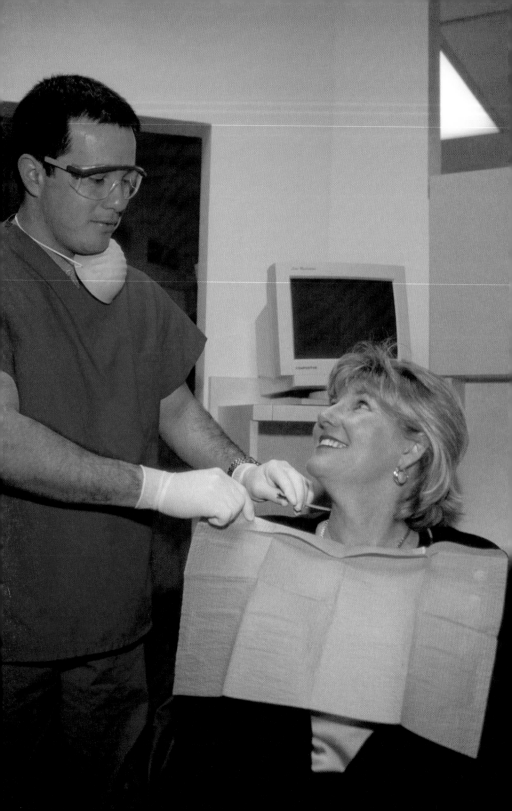

Related Careers

People interested in health or dental care have a variety of career opportunities. They may become physical therapy assistants or occupational therapy assistants. Physical therapy assistants help patients recover from injuries or medical conditions. Occupational therapy assistants help patients deal with physical limitations and perform everyday tasks.

People interested in health care careers also may become pharmacy technicians or veterinary technicians. Pharmacy technicians assist pharmacists in the preparation of medicines. Veterinary technicians help treat animals at veterinary clinics.

Today, people want strong, healthy teeth throughout their lives. Dental assistants will continue to play an important role in helping people maintain good dental health.

Dental assistants help people maintain good dental health.

Words to Know

bur (BUHR)—a cutting instrument placed in the end of a handpiece; patients commonly call this instrument a drill.

cavity (KAV-uh-tee)—a hole or hollow space in a tooth

dentures (DEN-churz)—a set of false teeth

handpiece (HAND-peess)—a long, thin instrument that dentists use to hold various instruments such as burs

hygiene (HYE-jeen)—actions people perform to stay clean and healthy; regularly brushing teeth is dental hygiene.

infectious disease (in-FEK-shuhss duh-ZEEZ)—a disease that can be passed from person to person

laboratory (LAB-ruh-tor-ee)—a room containing special equipment for dental assistants to use to perform certain tasks; dental assistants make casts of patients' teeth in a lab.

sterilize (STER-uh-lize)—to clean something so thoroughly that no germs or dirt remain; dental assistants sterilize dental instruments before they are used on patients.

x-ray (EKS-ray)—a photograph of a person's teeth and jaw bones

To Learn More

Cosgrove, Holli, ed. *Career Discovery Encyclopedia.* Vol. 2. 4th ed. Chicago: Ferguson Publishing, 2000.

Dofka, Charline M. *Competency Skills for the Dental Assistant.* Albany, N.Y.: Delmar Publishers, 1996.

Field, Shelly. *Career Opportunities in Health Care.* New York: Facts on File, 1997.

Kendall, Bonnie L. *Opportunities in Dental Care Careers.* VGM Opportunities. Lincolnwood, Ill.: VGM Career Horizons, 1991.

Simmers, Louise. *Diversified Health Occupations.* Albany, N.Y.: Delmar Publishers, 1998.

Useful Addresses

American Dental Assistants Association
203 North LaSalle Street
Suite 1320
Chicago, IL 60601-1225

Canadian Dental Assistants Association
105-1785 Alta Vista Drive
Ottawa, ON K1G 3Y6
Canada

Dental Assisting National Board
676 North Saint Clair
Suite 1880
Chicago, IL 60611

National Association of Dental Assistants
900 South Washington Street
Suite G-13
Falls Church, VA 22046

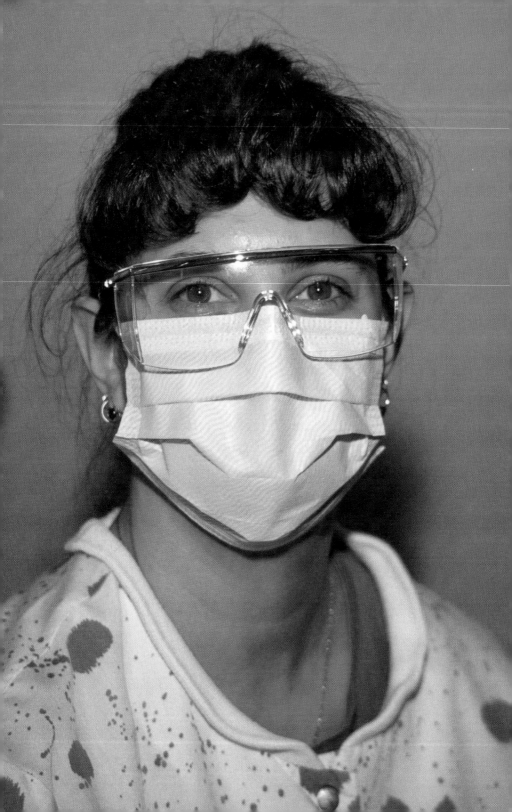

Internet Sites

American Dental Assistants Association
http://www.dentalassistant.org

American Student Dental Association
http://www.asdanet.org

The Canadian Dental Assistants' Association
http://www.cdaa.ca

Dental Assisting National Board
http://www.dentalassisting.com

Job Futures—Assisting Occupations in Support of Health Services
http://www.hrdc-drhc.gc.ca/corp/stratpol/arb/jobs/english/volume1/341/341.htm

Occupational Outlook Handbook— Dental Assistants
http://stats.bls.gov/oco/ocos163.htm

Index

advancement, 38–39
American Dental
    Assistants Association,
    32–33

bur, 12

Canadian Dental
    Assistants' Association,
    33
certification, 32
continuing education,
    32–33

Dental Assisting National
    Board (DANB), 31
dental hygienists, 25, 38
dentist, 7–8, 9, 11, 12–13,
    14, 17, 19–20, 25, 28,
    31, 35, 36, 38

education, 27–31, 35, 38
endodontics, 15

handpiece, 12

infectious disease, 14
instrument, 7–8, 12, 14,
    17–18, 19, 21

laboratory, 8
licensing, 31–32

National Dental Assisting
    Examining Board
    (NDAEB), 31–32

oral surgery, 15
orthodontics, 15
outlook, 35, 36–37

pediatric dentistry, 15

salary, 35–36

x-rays, 9–10, 11, 18, 25,
    31